PROMISES REVEALED

Life's Journey with God

JANET ANN SQUIRES

TRILOGY

Trilogy Christian Publishers
A Wholly Owned Subsidiary of Trinity Broadcasting Network
2442 Michelle Drive
Tustin, CA 92780

For information, address Trilogy Christian Publishing
Rights Department, 2442 Michelle Drive, Tustin, Ca 92780.
Trilogy Christian Publishing/ TBN and colophon are trademarks
of Trinity Broadcasting Network.
For information about special discounts for bulk purchases,
please contact Trilogy Christian Publishing.
Manufactured in the United States of America

10 9 8 7 6 5 4 3 2 1
Library of Congress Cataloging-in-Publication Data is available.
ISBN 978-1-63769-816-7
ISBN 978-1-63769-817-4 (ebook)

DEDICATION

I dedicate this book to my awesome husband, John Squires, Jr., who encouraged me to dream big dreams. To my girls, Breanna and Rachel, and my son-in-love, Caleb, words cannot describe how proud you make me. To my Aunt T for being my second mom. Amy, Doug, and Samantha you all make me smile every day and we share our lives and hearts together. To Anna and Bud McCartney thank you for our Godly heritage. To John and Dorothy Squires thank you for my hubby and your love. To David and Kristen, Jared and Christine, and Chelsie and Daniel Squires, I love you more than you could ever know. Taylor, Logan, and Alexa you are so wonderful, and I love you so much. My amazing group of lifelong friends. P.C., Andrea, Megan and Abby, Joy and Dave, Mason, Alexa, Carter, Tim and Katie, and Emily, Joey, Hudson, and Arianna. Without your challenging me and keeping me real I would not have even attempted this. Jason and Amanda, Adalynn and Audrey, because of you I have a Texas family. For Laura and Heather, without your friendship and laughs I would not make it through each day. To my co-workers, thank you for the laughs and encouraging me to improve myself every day. Pastor Robert and David Hogan because of your challenging words I must search deep to explore the promises written in this book. Thank you for being wonderful stewards of God's anointing and your pastoral responsibilities. To my Spring First Church Family I love doing life with you all. Charlotte Pyle thank you for being my cheerleader for any challenge.

TABLE OF CONTENTS

INTRODUCTION

———

THE WHY

Let me first tell you, thank you for taking the time to take this journey with me. I want to introduce myself to you. My name is Janet Squires, and I am a wife, mother, and RN, but foremost I am daughter of the God of the universe. I want you to know that I have approached this project with reverence and with a humble spirit. I have spent many days negotiating, well basically ignoring, the small voice inside of me that was asking me to take this leap of faith. Have you ever been there, or is it just me? In my own ability, I feel unworthy to do what God has asked me to do, but isn't that how God works? I find it funny that God often calls the ones who are the least qualified for the job. For example, He asked Moses to lead his people out of captivity, yet Moses had a stutter and God used his weakness and gave him a voice that saved a nation. God asked the daughter of a Jew to walk into the king's palace and find favor above all others, and through her wisdom and the prayer of her people. She saved a whole nation from genocide.

I am not calling what I am doing the same as saving a whole generation.

However, if my words can encourage just one of any generation to be reminded of what benefits, provision, and promises are found in being part of the God's family, then I count all the nights of unrest and the internal battle as joy. It has been difficult for me to allow God to have my hands and heart as I put pen to paper. The premise of this book is to remind you of the promises of God. I had a dream of a tree with a lion's face coming out of it. I felt it represents the heritage of God that is found within us, and that the tree symbolizes the followers of Christ. To endure the storm of life, we must have a deep-rooted knowledge of God's Word. So, when the storms come our way, we will come through them still standing. The Bible tells us: in:

> What delight comes to the one who follows God's ways! He won't walk in step with the wicked, nor share the sinner's way, nor be found sitting in the scorner's seat. His passion is to remain true to the Word of "I AM," meditating day and night on the true revelation of light. He will be standing firm like a flourishing tree planted by God's design, deeply rooted by the brooks of bliss, bearing fruit in every season of life. He is never dry, never fainting, ever blessed, ever prosperous.
>
> Psalms 1:1-3, TPT

I pray these verses over my children every morning that they will never faint and will ever be blessed and prosperous. My heart's deepest desire is that as you read this reminder your heart is stirred with the realization of how much God loves you. If we can just get a small glimpse of the love of the Father for us, then our whole countenance will change. I want the way you look at life to radically change as you view it through our Father's eyes

1.

THE PROMISE OF
FORGIVENESS

The promise of forgiveness is one of the most powerful promises found in God's Word. As we know, when there is discord of the heart or unforgiveness, it is as if chains are wrapped around you. Then you become captive and that unforgiveness turns into bitterness. The heart then has guilt entangled deep around your heart preventing you from loving where you need to. This unforgiveness is just a part of being human in an imperfect world. Today culture is full of those who are being offended. I think as the church we must learn to give grace and show love even when we feel others are wrong. One of my favorite stories in the Bible is of the prodigal son found in Luke 15. This chapter tells the story of a wealthy man who had two sons. One son asks for the portion of his inheritance and the father gives it to him. Then he leaves to go to a foreign country and he wastes it. Then suddenly he experiences a change in his condition and environment. Is that not just like we experienced with the introduction of one microscopically small virus bringing disruption and social unrest within a day? Within weeks everyone was in lockdown and our outlook for the future changed. So, this unknown prodigal went from a place of plenty to a place of devastation. When he hit the bottom, he was so hungry he would eat from where he was slopping the pigs. I think sometimes as Christians we have a prodigal mindset. We look around at our surroundings and think, *I am just going to keep working and do the best with my current situation,* thinking that our current situation is the best that God has for us. But let me challenge you: are you settling for the pigpen version of your life? The Bible tells us in Luke:

> But when he came to himself, he said, "How many of my father's hired servants have bread enough and to spare, and I perish with hunger! I will arise and go to my father, and will say to him, 'Father, I have sinned against heaven and before you, and I am no longer worthy to be called your son. Make me like one of your hired servants.'"

Luke 15:17-19, NKJV

So, he did just that; he went home where he knew the condition would be better. His father saw him from a far. *Do* you know what that means? It means he was looking for Him and anticipating His return. Luke 15:20 is beautiful. It tells us he rose and came to the Father. He then fell on his neck and kissed Him. There are seasons in our lives when we feel like we are far off. Is there a place or person where you need to ask for forgiveness and go home? We need to wake up to the reality that God is like that father watching for us to come home. Shake off the chains of unforgiveness, feeling you are not good enough or not worthy. There is always room for more.

I can only imagine that his father was constantly wondering and pondering what his son was doing and why he had not returned home. In the story, the son draws from the memory of how well he saw his father treat the servants in their home. I think this father is a perfect example of what our heavenly Father is like. He is kind and willing to accept all, no matter our status. God loves us and is waiting in anticipation for us to come to our senses and to run home. This son still had the stench of the pigpen and the dirt from travel. But the father ran to him and embraced him. He was joyful and immediately restored.

Did you catch that? Immediately restored. Forgiveness was given and he was made whole. Immediately upon our confession of sin God welcomes us home and restores us. God will take the dirt in and welcome us home with all of it. *He* does not expect us to change our ways and strive to be better before we come. He wants us to come just as we are, and He will help us with restoration. The journey with Christ starts with a confession. "If we confess our sins, he is faithful and righteous to forgive us our sins, and to cleanse us from all unrighteousness" (1 John 1:9, ASV). All it takes is a simple prayer. "Father, please forgive me for all my sins and cleanse my heart and I will follow you all the days of my life." It is that simple. The divine plan for forgiveness only comes through the saving grace of Jesus dying on the cross and raising to life again in three days. It is overwhelming to me in my simple and finite mind how God, Who spoke the world into existence, loves me so much He gave His one and only Son for me. So, the power of forgiveness not only applies to us through God's salvation, but it applies to us forgiving each other.

Let us be real, this one is easy for me to do for someone else's family. But if this affects me personally it often takes longer to forgive people who are near to us because their words and actions often wound us deeper. As a nurse, I have physically observed wounds healing in varying degrees over different amounts of time. Each layer of the skin heals from the inside out. If it heals only on the surface, the area underneath can become infected and it will ultimately break back open. When we extend forgiveness to others, the Lord will start working in us and allow us to completely heal without the potential for reinfection of unforgiveness and bitterness to enter back into the wound. That does not mean people will not hurt you or say mean things. It means that we are required to demonstrate love, patience, and gentleness. We must bestow God's love on them. You will see differently what used to cause you distress, disrupt your peace, and cause you to be unsettled in your heart. I can honestly say that the longer I serve Jesus, the more this holds true. This does not mean that I do not struggle.

Let me give you a real-life situation that I had to deal with. I went to LPN school straight after high school. I was one of two teenagers in the class of forty-five who were attending this program. The teacher made us stand up and actually belittled me and the other girl who were both only seventeen.

For the next nine months of school, she continued to point at us with any opportunity. I prayed and prayed a lot to hold my tongue and for the anger inside me to go away. I did not want the embarrassment and hurt that she had caused me to fester into bitterness and hate. So, I continued to work and be kind. I graduated in the top five of my class and the same teacher who had made fun of me became the teacher who had to pin me and present me with my diploma.

There are times when not well-meaning individuals speak those ugly words to me or about me. I must remember to pause and run and tell my heavenly Father, and hand the pain and anxiety over to Him. Just like a child tells their parent about the bully on the playground, this is the perfect example of how we need to run to our Father with our concerns. He cares about us. Our heavenly Father will kiss the hurt away and send us along with words of wisdom and feeling secure with the brush of His mighty hand. According to Galatians 5:22-23, "But the fruit of the Spirit is love, joy, peace, longsuffering, kindness, goodness, faithfulness, gentleness, self-control. Against such there is no law" (NKJV). The Holy Spirit is always working in your life if you allow Him to take part. He will encourage and give you guidance on how to navigate those difficult situations. There is absolutely no Christian who is perfect day in and day out. That is why the Bible tells us that His mercy is new every morning.

God knows His children so well that He knew we were going to need His daily forgiveness. Let us remember to always extend that grace to those around us. If we need to have daily forgiveness, should we not do the same for our neighbors, co-workers, and families? It is never too late, no matter how young or old you are. Jesus' compassion for us never fails. A tragic picture of the cross of calvary paints a bleak outlook for the thief on the cross who was guilty of the crime. In Luke 23, one was mocking Jesus but another recognized what a divine moment he had been destined to be a part of. He asked Jesus to remember him, and Jesus told him that he would be with Him in paradise. Who is He in your life? Do not wait until it is your final moment to ask Jesus into your heart. Jesus always is willing even in the final moment of your life to welcome you home. Do not wait. Make that decision today and learn to stand on the promises found in His Word.

If you need to make that decision today, it is as simple as saying the following:

Jesus, I come to you with all my faults and failures and ask You for forgiveness through the blood You shed on the cross on my behalf. I ask You to forgive me and I will live my life serving You. In Your name, Amen.

This is the simplest process but your life as a new creation in Christ started this very moment. Welcome to the family!

2.

THE PROMISE OF
PEACE

Some days when I am finished with my work, I realize I have not remembered to eat or take a minute to check on those that I love the most. Peace is often something we feel is not attainable. I am not saying we are not going to have struggles or difficulties. There will be times when the very core of our existence is shaken. What I am saying is even when those life-altering diagnoses come or accidents happen, there will be a peace that stirs up in your heart to remind you that you are not alone. Peace for me is knowing that no matter what situation I face, God is right there with me. He already notes the number of the days in my life. God knew the totality of my life before it began. *Strong's Concordance* defines peace as a harmonious state of soul and mind. The state of being both externally and internally calm. I think God sometimes looks at us and wonders, *why are you not asking for my help?* I remember when our girls were little, they would destroy our living room. I would tell them to clean up their mess. The complaining and whining would then commence but I found if I helped them, then the job of picking up their toys would be finished in just a few minutes and no one was left feeling frustrated or angry. I think God is waiting for us to ask Him for help. What room of your heart needs cleaning?

I have been in situations in my life where I felt that God was so distant from me. It was almost like I was inside of a glass, soundproof box. I could make my requests known but it was like I could not hear or feel the response. Let me give you one example from my personal experience. I have been working as a licensed practical nurse for years and I had the goal of advancing my career. To accomplish that goal, I had to go back to college to obtain my Associate's Degree. I completed the online classes and had incredibly good grades. I had to go to a testing site and take the clinical practicum to then get the remaining credits. I prepared and worked hard, but I failed the practicum and then all those classes became invaluable. I was devastated, and to be completely honest I was so mad at God. I could not understand why this would happen to me. Why? I prepared and was doing my best to serve God, *why did this not work out for me?*

My heart was wounded and very raw. I questioned everything I was ever taught about God. As I prepared to go to church that evening, I heard God speak to my heart to sing *God on the Mountain.* This is an old southern gospel song that many of you may not know. The chorus of this song says, "The God on the mountain is still the God of the valley and when things go wrong, He will make them right." I politely in my heart told God, "No, thank You, I do not want to sing about

Your goodness." Then the Holy Spirit began stirring in my heart and I knew I had to be obedient. Then within my spirit something reminded me that if we only believe God when all is well, then the depth of our Christian walk is shallow. I knew of the faithfulness of God; I just need to be reminded.

So, I took the stage that night still not convinced and not happy. As I sang the words of that chorus, I began to feel the oil of the Holy Spirit being poured out over me and the healing began. I do not know about you but when my heart is stressed and I am struggling to find peace, God often uses music to speak to me. I still do not understand why this all unfolded, but I can tell you that due to the detour I have three lifelong friends that I do not know I would have ever met. I am so glad God placed them in my life. We have journeyed through some great and some incredibly sad times. We are still friends over ten years later. I did get my Associate's Degree and then my Bachelor's while working full time. I can tell you that God is faithful and is close to us even we cannot feel He is there. Psalms 138:3 tells us, "At the very moment I called out to you, you answered me! You strengthened me deep within my soul and breathed fresh courage into me" (TPT). In Psalms 139:3-5, "You comprehend my path and my lying down, and are acquainted with all my ways. For there is not a word on my tongue, but behold, O Lord, You know it altogether. You have hedged me behind and before, and laid Your hand upon me" (NKJV).

Just remember that God knows every word that comes out

of your mouth. He knows the desires of your heart, even the ones you have not shared with a single person. He also cares about your disappointments, trials, and devastation. Just like earthly parents He sees your messy room and is willing to help you with the cleanup. There will be days you feel like you just stepped on a Lego and you'll stumble around in pain. But He will console you, help you through the painful situation, and send you back on your way. God knows your intimate pain and He wants to be the first person you run to with any situation. He has peace, joy, and direction waiting for you.

> On the same day, when evening had come, He said to them, "Let us cross over to the other side." Now when they had left the multitude, they took Him along in the boat as He was. And other little boats were also with Him. And a great windstorm arose, and the waves beat into the boat, so that it was already filling. But He was in the stern, asleep on a pillow. And they awoke Him and said to Him, "Teacher, do You not care that we are perishing?" Then He arose and rebuked the wind, and said to the sea, "Peace, be still!" And the wind ceased and there was a great calm.
>
> Mark 4:35-39, NKJV

Have you ever had a destination or goal for your life, and you were headed in that direction when out of nowhere the storm appeared and started to rock the situation? Was it the death of someone you loved? Was it the loss of a job? There will be times where the thunderstorms of life occur. There were no dark clouds of warning, the leaves on the tree did not turn backward, and the wind did not shift to give you any warning it was coming. Well, the storm does not surprise God. He knows. Do I understand why they occur? The answer to that is no. I will not ever attempt to explain to someone who has been through one of these storms "why" they come. When our lives are hit by these storms we sometimes wonder if God even cares about us. He does care. Even when we cannot explain the storm away, He is willing to be in the storm and intervene with comfort and peace. He can speak to the storm and have it ceased, or He will provide you the strength to reach the destination. What storm are you facing? Place it in the Master's hand.

3.

The Promise of
Restored Dreams

In 2 Kings we learn the story of a nameless woman.

> Now it happened one day that Elisha went to Shunem, where
> there was a notable woman, and she persuaded him to eat
> some food. So it was, as often as he passed by, he would turn
> in there to eat some food. And she said to her husband, "Look
> now, I know that this is a holy man of God, who passes by
> us regularly. Please, let us make [c]a small upper room on
> the wall; and let us put a bed for him there, and a table and
> a chair and a lampstand; so it will be, whenever he comes to
> us, he can turn in there.
>
> 2 Kings 4:8-10, NKJV

Do you ever feel that your identity is defined by where you
live, who you are married to, or what you do? I think we often
find ourselves in that situation. I am often John's wife or Bre
and Rachel's mom. I am also Nene to my niece and her friends.
One thing I am sure of is that when God looks at me, He sees all
of me and only me. He sees and knows every dream and deep

desire even when we do not share them with anyone else. The Bible tells us in Psalms 139:3-4, "You comprehend my path and my lying down, and are acquainted with all my ways. For there is not a word on my tongue, but behold, O Lord, You know it altogether" (NKJV).

So due to her kindness and generosity to the prophet of God, Gehazi, who was Elisha's servant, answered that she has no son and her husband is old. "So he said, 'Call her.' When he had called her, she stood in the doorway. Then he said, 'About this time next year you shall embrace a son.' And she said, 'No, my lord. Man of God, do not lie to your maidservant!'" (2 Kings 4:15-16, NKJV).

What a beautiful story of how her dream and desire that she obviously longed for was going to come to existence. What dream or calling is lying dormant in your womb? Is it a job you are called to transition to? Is there a ministry or charity in which you should be volunteering your time? Do you have hidden talents that only a few of your close family members or friends know about? When you finally do have the dream or are pursuing your calling, when tragedy hits what do you do? In this scripture, this beautiful story takes a very tragic turn.

And the child grew. Now it happened one day that he went out to his father, to the reapers. And he said to his father, "My head, my head!" So he said to a servant, "Carry him to his mother." When he had taken him and brought him to his mother, he sat on her knees till noon, and then died. And she went up and laid him on the bed of the man of God, shut the door upon him, and went out. Then she called to her husband, and said, "Please send me one of the young men and one of the donkeys, that I may run to the man of God and come back." So he said, "Why are you going to him today? It is neither the New Moon nor the Sabbath." And she said, "It is well." Then she saddled a donkey, and said to her servant, "Drive, and go forward; do not slacken the pace for me unless I tell you." And so she departed, and went to the man of God at Mount Carmel. So it was, when the man of God saw her afar off, that he said to his servant Gehazi, "Look, the Shunammite woman!"

2 Kings 4:18-25, NKJV

This is the part of the story that makes my heart shutter. In this story the woman's most precious request and deepest desire was to have a child. The Prophet of God spoke that over her life and her prayer was answered. I think oftentimes when we experience a miracle or a blessing that we feel we do not deserve we feel that is the end of the story. At times however, this story does not always play out as we thought it would. In this case, the child this woman had longed for passed away in her arms. I can barely fathom the pain and the questions running through her mind. What I love about this story is her relentless pursuit of holding onto the promise. Despite the outlook of what she could see as reality in front of her, she knew that if she connected with the man of God, it would change the situation, because God would intervene on her behalf. I love that in this part of the story this woman pursues a solution and she would not be stopped from where she was headed. I

25

love when she tells the servant to not slow the pace as she was going as hard as she physically could to get to the place of the life-changing encounter. When was the last time you pursued what God has told you to do with the passion and relentlessness of this woman? She was not going to stop until she had exhausted all efforts to restore her son. What is the restoration you are needing?

Now, let us finish the rest of the story.

So it was, when the man of God saw her afar off, that he said to his servant Gehazi, "Look, the Shunammite woman! Please run now to meet her, and say to her, 'Is it well with you? Is it well with your husband? Is it well with the child?'" And she answered, "It is well." Now when she came to the man of God at the hill, she caught him by the feet, but Gehazi came near to push her away. But the man of God said, "Let her alone; for her soul is in deep distress, and the Lord has hidden it from me, and has not told me." So she said, "Did I ask a son of my lord? Did I not say, 'Do not deceive me'?" Then he said to Gehazi, "Get yourself ready, and take my staff in your hand, and be on your way. If you meet anyone, do not greet him; and if anyone greets you, do not answer him; but lay my staff on the face of the child." And the mother of the child said, "As the Lord lives, and as your soul lives, I will not leave you." So he arose and followed her. Now Gehazi went on ahead of them, and laid the staff on the face of the child; but there was neither voice nor hearing. Therefore he went back to meet him, and told him, saying, "The child has not awakened." When Elisha came into the house, there was the child, lying dead on his bed. He went in therefore, shut the door behind the two of them, and prayed to the Lord. And he went up and lay on the child, and put his mouth on his mouth, his eyes on his eyes, and his hands on his hands; and he stretched himself out on the child, and the flesh of the child became warm. He returned and walked back and forth in the house, and again went up and stretched himself out on him; then the child sneezed seven times, and the child opened his eyes. And he called Gehazi and said, "Call this Shunammite woman." So he called her. And when she came in to him, he said, "Pick up your son." So she went in, fell at his feet, and bowed to the ground; then she picked up her son and went out.

2 Kings 4:25-37, NKJV

So, what I find fascinating about this Shunammite woman is at no time was she going to take less than the absolute best answer from this Prophet of God. She went with purpose and intent with an ask that she was determined would be the answer. I often struggle in my humanness to feel worthy enough to ask great requests of God. I will ask it on your behalf with all the faith in the world and never doubt that God's going to provide the solution to you. But when it comes to my personal walk, I often miss the fact that like this Shunammite woman, I did not ask for this blessing or this opportunity that has been presented

27

to me. But was it the intent of my heart to have it and so just like her we often are thankful for the blessing? However, when it does not seem to go the way we want it to, that is when the struggle begins. This is one of my favorite stories in the Bible for a couple of reasons. One, I love stories of incredible women who do amazing things for God. Second, this woman had a tenacity that I admire.

Today we are often taught as women to not be powerful and to silence our voices. But what I want to say is, God is no respecter of person, race, or ethnicity. He wants to hear *your* voice. He wants to hear *your* passion. He wants you to be relentless in your pursuit of the dreams that He has placed inside of you. He wants you to do what He has called you to do. We often think that the job of the pastor, evangelist, prophet, or teacher has a higher calling than the job of a stay-at-home mom, or a nurse at the bedside of a patient, or a CNA in a nursing home. All members of the body are vital members of the Kingdom of God. You are called to transform whatever and wherever God has placed you for this season of your life. Is it by a word of encouragement? I often find myself discovering the opportunity to encourage someone. It starts with just being observant, looking at someone's eyes or watching their countenance when they enter a room. Taking the time to see how they carry themselves. What is one act of kindness or blessing you could bestow on someone to change their life? In this story, the Shunammite woman did an act of service for Elisha. He met her longest unspoken request.

In verse 29 Elisha gives direction to Gehazi to take his staff and place it knowing this child in proxy of him going. The Mama in the story was having no part of it. She told Elisha that she was not going to leave him. I think of this in two different ways. The first is that she had a child who was dead, and she was not going to allow that situation to continue on behalf of her child. So, let me stop right here and encourage you if you have a child who is away from the calling that God placed on them, or is struggling with how to walk it out, has the enemy put them in bondage and chains, and you feel like there is no hope? In the spiritual world this child is dead to the things that God has called them to do. Let me remind you of the Shunammite woman who saw her dead child, but she was not going to allow that to be the outcome.

So, when you are going before God's throne and advocating for the child, see the outcome you want. You can say, "Lord, I do not understand. I do not see what You are seeing but I trust Your outcome and call for my children." The one thing that holds true is the same God that allowed Elisha to raise this unnamed child is the same God that will change the circumstance for my child and bring life to them spiritually again. The story does not get to end with the death of your child. The story does not get to end with them falling away. They will not be lost in addiction. They will not be entangled in whatever chains Satan has placed on them. I know that often we struggle with what we cannot see. Faith must take place of the evidence of things not yet seen and this is where the foundation of knowing what

God's Word says. This is where knowing that His promises are yes and Amen for His children. This makes all the difference to the outcome of our lives. Do not take a generic substitute for the genuine presence of the Lord.

I know we all love to go to church, and we love to feel the presence of God. Some of the most genuine times in my life when I have felt the presence of God work the most intimately, I had no words to speak except to call out for Jesus. I would tell Him, "I can't do this without You, and I don't know what this is going to look like, but I am trusting You despite what I see." The one thing I know is true is God is faithful. I do not know about your situation. I do not know what you are experiencing in your life but that one thing I know is true. When the journey looks the darkest and you cannot see the light, allow God to walk the journey with you, trust His direction. Tell Him, "I don't know what the outcome is, but I know You have a plan and a purpose and a destination for my child." Faith in action is not always easy and to be quite honest there are times I do not understand life at all. I question Christians who say they never struggle. I do not feel that is authentic. We are human and full of emotion and struggles but that is the beautiful part of God. He knows and loves us despite our weaknesses. He understands that He just wants a real raw authentic communication of who you are. He loves you. When the Shunammite woman was asked by Elisha's servant, "Is it well with you?" She answered, "It is well." That was her faith in action. In the physical, she knew that she left at home her child on a bed with no life in him. But she knew in her heart if she connected herself with the God of all creation through this man of God, her son would live again.

Let us unpack the next part of the story. So, Elisha realizes very quickly that the Shunammite woman was not taking any substitution for his presence. I think that is powerful. Do not take the substitution of God's presence. Do not let anyone distract you from what you know God has told you to do. I believe the Shunammite woman knew that her only solution was to connect that prophet to her son. She knew that by Elisha coming a miracle would happen when Elisha went to the very room that the Shunammite woman in her kindness had created for him to rest. I often find it ironic that God sometimes takes you back to that very spot where your journey first started, to show you the entire story. I think He will often allow us to see how He orchestrated the steps even when we could not see. Even when we did not know one step leads to the other.

He did so when Elisha when laid himself on the child the first time nothing happened. I cannot imagine the agony the mother was going through at this time. But the second time the child sneezed and was restored to life. When the Shunammite woman entered that room, Elisha told her to take her son but the first thing she did was bow down and give thanks. Are you thankful when the answer comes? Do we have an opportunity to have a more grateful heart? I know that I have been given handfuls of blessings. Do I have a thankful heart? Thanksgiving is not just a holiday. Thanksgiving should be a lifestyle.

We should be thankful for each blessing small and great. I love it in the middle of the workday when I get a text from a friend or co-worker with encouragement. I love that God has prompted them to think of me. Or when God places someone on your heart, do you respond? Are you obedient? I think as I travel for work one thing I find true is a smile or kindness; giving somebody your spot in a line. Or giving up your first-class seat for coach so they can sit by their spouse. Are you being a great example of the love of the Father to those around you?

I want my heavenly Father to look down and say, "That was good. You did well today, Janet." Just like when my kids do something that just amazes me. I tell them how proud I am of them. God wants to help restore your dreams despite what you see in front of you. You may not see the big picture today. We may not even see it before we get to heaven. God is the same yesterday, today, and forever. He is orchestrating your life story out with intimate intricate detail. He loves you so much He weaves each part of it together. We often do not understand the color theme He is picking for this masterpiece, but the Artist always knows what the result will be. He encourages on those days that do not seem fair. Or when you are questioning what is going on with your child, finances, jobs, etc.

As you reflect on the passage found in 2 Kings 4, and read about the Shunammite woman, remind yourself of these things. Kindness and obedience to God's voice will place you in a position for blessings. God wants to see your relentless passion in prayer as you advocate for those whose situation does not look like you think it should. Thirdly, the situation when God steps in always changes, and what looks like death today will look like life restored tomorrow. What are the promises you need to be restored? When did you and God last have your conversation about that intimate part of your life? Are you praying and fasting and being relentless like the Shunammite woman? Are you pursuing the answer with the pace of this woman until you get the victory?

4.

The Promise of Friendship

A friend loves at all times, and a brother is born for adversity.

Proverbs 17:17, NKJV

I can honestly say that one thing I value in life as one the highest treasures I have is my friends. I love that I have people who surround me and keep me grounded and authentic. There is nothing better than a friend who knows the good, the bad, and the ugly and still loves you despite all of it. Did you know that before Adam and Eve messed up so royally they would have direct in-person communication with God? Genesis 3:8, "And they heard the sound of the Lord God walking in the garden in the cool of the day, and Adam and his wife hid themselves from the presence of the Lord God among the trees of the garden" (NKJV). I take this verse to mean they knew the sound of God walking toward them. That day, however, was different because they had eaten of the forbidden fruit they had been instructed not to and they were ashamed. That day the division between God and man to have intimate and direct contact stopped due to disobedience. That intimate contact was restored on the day Jesus died on the cross. Giving us back direct contact through the blood covenant we once again have direct access to interact with Him through prayer and conversation. I am so thankful for this.

In the book of Ruth, it tells us the story of Naomi, who was a wife, and she had two sons and two daughters-in-law. Naomi's husband and both of her sons passed away. Naomi then tells her daughters-in-law to go home to their parents so they may find husbands and be cared for. Naomi was going to return to Moab because she had heard of God's blessing on that land. But Ruth would not leave her. In chapter 1 Ruth said:

> "Entreat me not to leave you, *Or to* turn back from following after you; For wherever you go, I will go; And wherever you lodge, I will lodge; Your people *shall be* my people, And your God, my God. Where you die, I will die, And there will I be buried. The Lord do so to me, and more also, If *anything but* death parts you and me." When she saw that she was determined to go with her, she stopped speaking to her.
>
> Ruth 1:16-18, NKJV

Ruth and Naomi returned to Moab in the harvest time. Ruth asked to glean in the fields and Boaz, who was a very wealthy landowner, found favor with her. He instructed his servants to allow her to glean in the fields and give her extra so she would always have enough.

> So she fell on her face, bowed down to the ground, and said to him, "Why have I found favor in your eyes, that you should take notice of me, since I am a foreigner?" And Boaz answered and said to her, "It has been fully reported to me, all that you have done for your mother-in-law since the death of your husband, and how you have left your father and your mother and the land of your birth, and have come to a people whom you did not know before. The Lord repay your work, and a full reward be given you by the Lord God of Israel, under whose wings you have come for refuge."
>
> Ruth 2:10-12, NKJV

The part of the story that touches my heart the most is that Ruth was not thinking of herself when she took the commitment to follow Naomi to a place she had never known. She took the commitment to be a friend regardless of the situation, without regard for her own comfort or future. I think the Bible gives us this description of what friendship should look like because sometimes friendship is hard. We must be committed to those we love. I think as Christians we often say, "Yeah, I love you," but it stops with the words. It is when the going gets tough that I think we have the greatest opportunity to affect those around us. When the job is gone and when the death comes unexpectedly or just a tragedy that hits us out of nowhere, we need to be there when our friends need us the most.

Nothing ever surprises God. You did not catch him off guard. He knew about the loss of a job or the challenge you are facing. The God of the universe, He was there before time began and He is there when time ends. I think we often try to put God in the space of our human minds and there is no time or space for God.

As the story continues, Boaz makes Ruth his wife and restores her, and this is the foretelling of the story of Jesus being our kinsman Redeemer that even when we were not deserving, or from a strange land, or even when we are in living in sin God loved us enough to send His Son to be our Redeemer to give us salvation that we did not deserve.

I am very blessed to have some lifelong friends who have walked some crazy journeys with me. In the Bible there is another story about four friends who carry an extremely ill man to see Jesus. They take him to be healed and, in this story, they cannot get him to Jesus but then something happens.

Then behold, men brought on a bed a man who was paralyzed, whom they sought to bring in and lay before Him. And when they could not find how they might bring him in, because of the crowd, they went up on the housetop and let him down with his bed through the tiling into the midst before Jesus. When He saw their faith, He said to him, "Man, your sins are forgiven you." And the scribes and the Pharisees began to reason, saying, "Who is this who speaks blasphemies? Who can forgive sins but God alone?" But when Jesus perceived their thoughts, He answered and said to them, "Why are you reasoning in your hearts? Which is easier, to say, 'Your sins are forgiven you,' or to say, 'Rise up and walk'? But that you may know that the Son of Man has power on earth to forgive sins"—He said to the man who was paralyzed, "I say to you, arise, take up your bed, and go to your house." Immediately he rose up before them, took up what he had been lying on, and departed to his own house, glorifying God. And they were all amazed, and they glorified God and were filled with fear, saying, "We have seen strange things today!"

Luke 5:18-26, NKJV

I love the story of this friendship found in these verses. The friends knew they had to get this paralyzed man in front of Jesus and when they got there, they could not get to Him. It would have been extremely easy for them to turn around and go home. But I love that they were not going to take what they saw as an obstacle to prevent their friend from getting what he needed from Jesus. His friends went up on the rooftop and made a hole to lower this man down through. Do you have the blessing of a friend who will lead you to Jesus? Are you willing enough to be a friend who will remove obstacles from people's lives to get them in front of Jesus? I know I have friends who, when I struggle or am discouraged, encourage me through God's Word, and they pray for me and fast on my behalf. I think this is a great description of how the body of

Christ should work when one is weak and cannot get where they need to be: that we carry them there. I am sure it was not convenient for these men to bring this paralyzed man that day to Jesus. It would have been quite easy for them to just go and listen to the teacher.

This man's life was changed. He was completely restored because of the work of these men. I believe not only did the paralyzed man get a miracle, but those friends who brought him there also had a life-changing encounter with Jesus. They were able to see firsthand that when He speaks life to you the situation immediately changes.

Let me tell you about my circle for a minute. First, I have my sister who is my ride or die. She loves me, encourages me, and calls me out. My life is richer because of her. My sister would move heaven and earth for me or my family, and I would do the same for her. Next is my circle five lifelong friends. We may be miles apart but when one of us has a need, another will immediately intercede with Jesus on their behalf. Friendship is not a relationship we should feel is disposable. Lifelong friendships are formed over countless years and experiences, through joy, tears, trials, and victories. The most beautiful and valued friendships I have stood the test of time. They have not been perfect, but they are precious, and I would not trade the world for any of them. Each phone call, each visit is special and unique, and God blesses us with the opportunity to have friendship and community. I believe it was His vision for what the Garden of Eden was meant to be communing friend to friend. To have great friends you need to be a great friend. Send that card, send those flowers, look for a unique gift. Go out of your way for people. Jesus did. Let me challenge you: who are your friends that you have today who need you to help them remove obstacles in their lives to get them to Jesus? Are you willing to make that sacrifice as a friend?

5.

THE PROMISE OF
INTERRUPTION

Webster's Dictionary defines interruption as a stoppage or hindering of an activity for a time. I often find that some of the greatest moments in my life have occurred because of an interruption. In the life of Jesus recorded in the gospels, it refers frequently to interruptions. Jesus has often been bombarded by people who needed something from Him. They knew that Jesus held healing in life and He could speak of things yet to come. I think Jesus was a people person and that people were drawn to Him because He cared and had such compassion for those around Him. I think we often go through our daily lives not wanting interruptions, but who has God placed in your path today for you to change their destiny?

Luke 8 tells us two stories:

So it was, when Jesus returned, that the multitude welcomed Him, for they were all waiting for Him. And behold, there came a man named Jairus, and he was a ruler of the synagogue. And he fell down at Jesus' feet and begged Him to come to his house, for he had an only daughter about twelve years of age, and she was dying. But as He went, the multitudes thronged Him. Now a woman, having a flow of blood for twelve years, who had spent all her livelihood on physicians and could not be healed by any, came from behind and touched the border of His garment. And immediately her flow of blood stopped. And Jesus said, "Who touched Me?" When all denied it, Peter and those with him said, "Master, the multitudes throng and press You, and You say, 'Who touched Me?' " But Jesus said, "Somebody touched Me, for I perceived power going out from Me." Now when the woman saw that she was not hidden, she came trembling; and falling down before Him, she declared to Him in the presence of all the people the reason she had touched Him and how she was healed immediately. And He said to her, "Daughter, be of good cheer; your faith has made you well. Go in peace." While He was still speaking, someone came from the ruler of the synagogue's house, saying to him, "Your daughter is dead. Do not trouble the Teacher." But when Jesus heard it, He answered him, saying, "Do not be afraid; only believe, and she will be made well." When He came into the house, He permitted no one to go in except Peter, James, and John, and the father and mother of the girl. Now all wept and mourned for her; but He said, "Do not weep; she is not dead, but sleeping." And they ridiculed Him, knowing that she was dead. But He put them all outside, took her by the hand and called, saying, "Little girl, arise." Then her spirit returned, and she arose immediately.

And He commanded that she be given something to eat. And her parents were astonished, but He charged them to tell no one what had happened.

Luke 8:40-56, NKJV

Have you ever been so desperate for an answer from God that you would be almost to the point of being rude or pushy to get to Jesus? I love the tenacity of this woman who once again goes unnamed in this passage. I can picture this so vividly in my mind. She was so desperate. She was out of money, out of resources, out of hope. She saw the opportunity for her life to be transformed and she pushed her way through all the crowd to touch Jesus' garment. She knew by connecting to Him her life would be changed. I know we know that, but how often do we stay in our seats and carry our burdens in and out of the church? How often do we feel that our need is too small or possibly too insignificant to present to God? I love this lady. She had the drive to set apart the restriction of the day because in this culture she would have been an outcast. She would have been considered unclean. In this story her faith caused a scene to occur. It caused Jesus to stop and take notice of her. Do you want Jesus to stop and take notice of your faith? I certainly do. Her life depended on her connecting to Jesus. Do not let others stand in the way of your miracle. Grab hold of the promises in His Word.

Now the scene flashes to Jairus. I wonder if he was aggravated by the unnamed woman's healing. I wonder if he was discouraged by the delay of the answer. Have you ever been there when you thought the answer was coming but then it was delayed? Have you been in a place of desperation and saw others receive their blessing, but you did not receive your answer when you felt you should? I am almost positive this father was questioning why this woman had interrupted Jesus getting to his daughter. This is where as the parent I would have been terribly angry, possibly hysterical, due to someone delaying Jesus from my answer. But one thing we miss is how big God is and He is everywhere we need Him, whenever we call. He is not controlled by time and space.

Jairus then got the report that his little girl was dead. Jesus corrected him and said, "She is just sleeping." I think there is a very deep truth found in this passage. Your spiritual vision must align with the Bible, what your prayer life indicates, and what God is telling you. I love when Jesus arrives, He does not permit everyone to be in the room. Who are you allowing in your circle that could be distracting you from the promise that is set before you? When Jesus speaks, He restores life back to the little girl. Can you imagine being outside of the room and hearing this little girl's feet hit the floor? Be careful who you surround yourself with. Are they lifting you up? Are they encouraging you? Do they push you to access Jesus?

I am so thankful to have friends that encourage me to seek God for every life decision I must face. They challenge me to be the best to those around me. What room of your heart or situation do you need Jesus to speak to? What do you need to have brought back to life? There will be people at times who will laugh at you when you share with them what God has told you. When you know that you know, do not let anyone plant the seed of doubt in your heart. If God told you it will come to pass you may not be able to see the whole journey but keep on walking. The most impactful part of this story for me is that truth when Jesus walks into the room. It does not matter who else is there. When He speaks something no one or nothing can change it. Just remember, if Jesus is present with you in the room the prayer will be answered according to His perfect will.

6.

THE PROMISE OF
PREPARATION

———

Do you ever feel like you are on a constant hamster wheel of always getting prepared for the next thing? I think that's God's way of keeping us humble for the next journey or challenge that life is going to throw at us. Webster's Dictionary defines preparation as the act of being prepared for a particular purpose, use, or service. When I think of Bible characters that perfectly describe preparation for the job ahead, I have two specifically in mind. The first is an innocent fourteen-year-old girl who was found to be perfect in God's sight and was asked to carry God's Son. The second is David, and boy did he have a lot of mess-ups. I think he is a perfect example of God's willingness to use anyone and make them a vessel He can use to change the world.

> Now in the sixth month the angel Gabriel was sent by God to a city of Galilee named Nazareth, to a virgin betrothed to a man whose name was Joseph, of the house of David. The virgin's name *was* Mary. And having come in, the angel said to her, "Rejoice, highly favored *one*, the Lord is with you;

blessed are you among women!" But when she saw *him*, she was troubled at his saying, and considered what manner of greeting this was. Then the angel said to her, "Do not be afraid, Mary, for you have found favor with God. And behold, you will conceive in your womb and bring forth a Son, and shall call His name Jesus. He will be great, and will be called the Son of the Highest; and the Lord God will give Him the throne of His father David. And He will reign over the house of Jacob forever, and of His kingdom there will be no end." Then Mary said to the angel, "How can this be, since I do not know a man?" And the angel answered and said to her, "*The* Holy Spirit will come upon you, and the power of the Highest will overshadow you; therefore, also, that Holy One who is to be born will be called the Son of God. Now indeed, Elizabeth your relative has also conceived a son in her old age; and this is now the sixth month for her who was called barren. For with God nothing will be impossible." Then Mary said, "Behold the maidservant of the Lord! Let it be to me according to your word." And the angel departed from her.

Luke 1:26-38, NKJV

I cannot imagine being young, unmarried, and never knowing a man and an Angel comes to me and asks me to carry God's child. What a great responsibility to not only be a mother at such a young age, but also the mother of God. Take a minute let that sink in: the God of creation living in your womb. God who loved us enough to take the glory of heaven off and take human form to bring us back into full communion with Him through the salvation plan of the cross. The power of preparation is no more exemplified in the journey of Mary carrying baby Jesus to birth. I have had the privilege of carrying two children in my body and there is no greater profound responsibility for the mother. Everything that you consume, that you feel, that you do has to be considered to ensure the safety and well-being of the baby that is developing inside of you. The Bible does not tell us a lot about Jesus' developmental years. As a matter of fact, it tells us close to nothing until we see Jesus in the temple around twelve years of age speaking in ways that baffle the high priest of the time. I wonder what it was like teaching Jesus to walk, and teaching Him how to talk, and disciplining Him when He was going to get into something that he should not have. I think sometimes we get frustrated with the waiting process that occurs as God prepares us for what is next. In natural childbirth, there's pain associated with the delivery process. It cannot be avoided; that is the way it must occur.

I think sometimes we feel that we should live a life free of pain and suffering and trials. We want the baby, but we often do not want the growth pains that come with the growth of the dream, the vision, or the calling that God placed in our lives. We want the reward, but we often do not want to work. Jesus and Mary's journey was not an easy one. It was full of ridicule, feeling alone in their hometown, and having to make a great journey just to have no place to stay. I think it just shows the humanity of God to allow His Son who was there at the beginning of time to be born in human form in a stable among animals with stench and not in the best of situations. I'm sure Mary was scared. I'm sure she was exhausted as she travailed in a room that as a nurse I would not even feel would be appropriate to deliver a child in. There was no incubator, no sterile procedure, no medication—just her and Joseph delivering baby Jesus. When you look around at your situation, do you sometimes wonder how you got here? Is this what your life was supposed to look like? Is this where you thought you would be? When you look at your children do you wonder what is next for them? What does God have in store? Who is their spouse going to be?

In the story of the birth of Jesus, it was orchestrated exactly the way God had planned it out to fulfill the prophecies written by the prophets of the Old Testament. Your story is being written to fulfill the plan that God has for those that you are to influence in your life. Is that your co-workers, your neighbors, or your family? Do not let the stench of the situation prevent you from seeing the majesty of the plan. When the wise men came to worship, and the magi came from afar bearing gifts, they had the realization of who this little baby was. Let God birth in your heart the realization of who you are in Him. Do not allow your circumstances to dictate to you that God does not have a plan and purpose for this season of your life.

In Proverbs 16:19 it says within your heart you can make

plans for your future, but the Lord chooses the steps you take. When God has a plan and a purpose for your life and you're in tune with what He's asking you to do, He's going to orchestrate the steps that you must take. He's going to orchestrate that there will be a room in an inn when you need it. He will have the magi come from afar and He'll prepare the shepherds in a field. Hold on to the dream and the purpose and the calling that God has placed inside of you. The area of preparation is moving you toward what is next. The next part of your ministry, the next job that God has for you, the next community in which you will make a change.

Now we all know the story of David slaying Goliath and how he was not going to allow this giant to mock the God that He served but this is just one part of the story of King David. One thing I love about this story is when the Prophet came to anoint the next King, David's dad did not even present him. He presented all his other brothers and as the Prophet kept saying, "Nope, not this one. Nope. not this one," he finally asked him if he had any other sons. And that is when, only after prompting, did he say, "Oh I have David, but he is in the field tending the sheep."

In 1 Samuel 16:13, Samuel took the horn of oil and anointed him in the presence of his brothers, and from that day on the spirit of the Lord came powerfully upon David. Long before David sat on a throne he tended to sheep in the field. So, let us look at the story found in 1 Samuel 17:

Then Jesse said to his son David, "Take now for your brothers an ephah of this dried *grain* and these ten loaves, and run to your brothers at the camp. And carry these ten cheeses to the captain of *their* thousand, and see how your brothers fare, and bring back news of them." Now Saul and they and all the men of Israel were in the Valley of Elah, fighting with the Philistines. So David rose early in the morning, left the sheep with a keeper, and took *the things* and went as Jesse had commanded him. And he came to the camp as the army was going out to the fight and shouting for the battle. For Israel and the Philistines had drawn up in battle array, army against army. And David left his supplies in the hand of the supply keeper, ran to the army, and came and greeted his brothers. Then as he talked with them, there was the champion, the Philistine of Gath, Goliath by name, coming up from the armies of the Philistines; and he spoke according to the same words. So David heard *them*. And all the men of Israel, when they saw the man, fled from him and were dreadfully afraid. So the men of Israel said, "Have you seen this man who has come up? Surely he has come up to defy Israel; and it shall be that the man who kills him the king will enrich with great riches, will give him his daughter, and give his father's house exemption *from taxes* in Israel." Then David spoke to the men who stood by him, saying, "What shall be done for the man who kills this Philistine and takes away the reproach from Israel? For who is this uncircumcised Philistine, that he should defy the armies of the living God?" And the people answered him in this manner, saying, "So shall it be done for the man who kills him." Now Eliab his oldest brother heard when he spoke to the men; and Eliab's anger was aroused against David, and he said, "Why did you come down here? And with whom have you left those few sheep in the wilderness? I know your pride and the insolence of your heart, for you have come down to see the battle." And David said, "What have I done now? *Is there* not a cause?" Then he turned from him toward another and said the same thing; and these people answered him as the first ones *did*. Now when the words which David spoke were heard, they reported *them* to Saul; and he sent for him. Then David said to Saul, "Let no man's heart fail because of him; your servant will go and fight with this Philistine." And Saul said to David, "You are not able to go against this Philistine to fight with him; for you *are* a youth, and he a man of war from his youth." But David said to Saul, "Your servant used to keep his father's sheep, and when a lion or a bear came and took a lamb out of the flock, I went out after it and struck it, and delivered *the lamb* from its mouth; and when it arose against me, I caught *it* by its beard, and struck and killed it. Your servant has killed both lion and bear; and this uncircumcised Philistine will be like one of them, seeing he has defied the armies of the living God." Moreover David said, "The Lord, who delivered me from the paw of the lion and from the paw of the bear, He will deliver me from the hand of this Philistine." And Saul said to David, "Go, and the Lord be with you!"

1 Samuel 17:17-37, NKJV

Let us take a few minutes to talk about the first part of this amazing story. When David was following the direction of his father, his brothers are kind of nasty, and ungrateful that he had traveled a long way to bring them supplies. They were unhappy that he would have the willingness and this spiritual boldness to say that the Philistines had no right to talk to them that way. I have to wonder as David was in the field tending the sheep, and as you know the bear would attack and the lion came for the sheep, if the same power that rose up in him to question the Philistine was the same power that had the small boy challenge the bear and the lion for the safety of the of the flock. God was preparing his next battle by giving him battles with the animals before he faced the giant.

I can personally attest that during the battles I have faced I have become frustrated with God, at times wondering why this is the battle I'm fighting. But with any warrior the battle of today is preparing you for the battle of tomorrow because as you rise in rank, or have greater responsibility, the battle becomes bigger. There are greater consequences with an outcome that affects more people. As we strive for the promotion, for the next job, or the next position or degree, I often think that we do not consider with greater responsibility comes greater accountability to those that are entrusted into your leadership.

I think as David was in the field having communion with

God and developing his spiritual man, God was developing his physical man for the battle that was about to be presented to him. I am sure on the day that David went to get the loaves and the grains to take to his brother he did not think that day was his day of destiny. I am sure he did not feel that he would be taking five smooth stones and putting them into a slingshot when King Saul had presented him his armor. One of the things I love about this story is David wanted to know what the reward was going to be for the battle he was going to partake in. God always shares with us the rewards. They're found in His Word. If you are questioning the benefits of serving God you just need to open His Book: they are "yes" and "amen" to those who love Him. Do not allow the voices of those around you to place doubt, mock you, or challenge your dreams or abilities. You plus God always equals victory, that is a powerful revelation when you can lay hold on that. David's brothers and those around him were not encouraging him; they were laughing at him and telling them that he was too little and should go back home where he belonged in the field. Someone else does not get to determine your seat for destiny. God determined your seat at the table.

Now let us pick up with the story in 1 Samuel 17:38:

So Saul clothed David with his armor, and he put a bronze helmet on his head; he also clothed him with a coat of mail. David fastened his sword to his armor and tried to walk, for he had not tested *them*. And David said to Saul, "I cannot walk with these, for I have not tested *them*." So David took them off. Then he took his staff in his hand; and he chose for himself five smooth stones from the brook, and put them in a shepherd's bag, in a pouch which he had, and his sling was in his hand. And he drew near to the Philistine. So the Philistine came, and began drawing near to David, and the man who bore the shield *went* before him. And when the Philistine looked about and saw David, he disdained him; for he was *only* a youth, ruddy and good-looking. So the Philistine said to David, "*Am* I a dog, that you come to me with sticks?" And the Philistine cursed David by his gods. And the Philistine said to David, "Come to me, and I will give your flesh to the birds of the air and the beasts of the field!" Then David said to the Philistine, "You come to me with a sword, with a spear, and with a javelin. But I come to you in the name of the Lord of hosts, the God of the armies of Israel, whom you have defied. This day the Lord will deliver you into my hand, and I will strike you and take your head from you. And this day I will give the carcasses of the camp of the Philistines to the birds of the air and the wild beasts of the earth, that all the earth may know that there is a God in Israel. Then all this assembly shall know that the Lord does not save with sword and spear; for the battle is the Lord's, and He will give you into our hands."

So it was, when the Philistine arose and came and drew near to meet David, that David hurried and ran toward the army to meet the Philistine. Then David put his hand in his bag and took out a stone; and he slung it and struck the Philistine in his forehead, so that the stone sank into his forehead, and he fell on his face to the earth. So David prevailed over the Philistine with a sling and a stone, and struck the Philistine and killed him. But *there was* no sword in the hand of David. Therefore David ran and stood over the Philistine, took his sword and drew it out of its sheath and killed him, and cut off his head with it. And when the Philistines saw that their champion was dead, they fled.

1 Samuel 17:38-51, NKJV

Oh, there is so much I love about this story. I love the tenacity of this young shepherd boy who had the boldness to stand when no one else did. Have you ever been in this situation when you were the only one that seemed to be doing the right thing? It is not an extremely comfortable place to be. I love that he knew the God he served so well that he knew if he stepped out to fight the battle there was no way he was going to fail. When was the last time you knew without a shadow of doubt in your heart that God had spoken to you? That you were in the right place at the right time and nothing that anyone else said or did was going to change your mind from the destiny and the calling that God placed on you? I have grown up in church all my life and one thing I know to be true is that often we choose to disqualify someone based on age or years of service for better words instead of the God that is inside of them. Shame on us if we disqualify someone by their appearance, their age, or even maybe the task that God is asking them to do. Do not allow yourself to become a critical Christian. Do not be that person. Do not be the brother of David who looked at his size or his job or his ability instead of seeing his anointing.

I love the boldness of David in the story. Not only did he prepare to fight a seasoned warrior, he ran to the battle. That is absolute confidence that he knew God had his back regardless. Do you know that? If we know that and if we live that how differently would our lives look every single day? When you get up in the morning and you prepare for your work would your attitude be better? Our presence should change the environment when we enter a room. God will provide you the tools you need for the battle. There were five smooth stones in a slingshot when the world felt that he needed a full armor customized for him from a King. All he needed was a shepherd's bag that had smooth stones in it and a slingshot. Use the tools God has presented to you. Do not look for someone else's gifting or calling. God has uniquely designed you for the task that He has placed for you to do. He has equipped you with your own shepherd's bag. It may not be a bag that has talents that are going to put you on a stage or put you in front of people. It may be a gifting of encouragement where no one ever knows what you're doing it for. God sees and God rewards. You may be the person who is able to look with the Father's compassion and love someone that others feel is unlovable or not worthy to be loved. If compassion is in your toolbox or in your shepherd's bag let God cultivate those giftings within you to change the world. Don't be afraid of the preparation for the next task. Enjoy your time in the field with the sheep while God's preparing you for the battlefield.

Another gem I gleaned from this story: David did not wear King Saul's armor. Why? It was not made for him. Are you trying to live someone else's calling? Are you uncomfortable with the position you are in? Is it because you are out of line with what God has for you? Just like when we put on a little weight, the shirt and pants, or your favorite dress does not fit quite right. Ensure you are seeking God's voice to walk out the journey He has specifically designed for you.

7.

THE PROMISE OF POWER

———

A s we look at all the promises found in God's Word, one of the most important for me is the Holy Spirit.

> Then He said to them, "These *are* the words which I spoke to you while I was still with you, that all things must be fulfilled which were written in the Law of Moses and *the* Prophets and *the* Psalms concerning Me." And He opened their understanding, that they might comprehend the Scriptures. Then He said to them, "Thus it is written, and thus it was necessary for the Christ to suffer and to rise from the dead the third day, and that repentance and remission of sins should be preached in His name to all nations, beginning at Jerusalem. And you are witnesses of these things. Behold, I send the Promise of My Father upon you; but tarry in the city of Jerusalem until you are endued with power from on high."
>
> Luke 24:44-49, NKJV

This is Jesus speaking to the disciples before His final ascension to heaven.

When the Day of Pentecost had fully come, they were all with one accord in one place. And suddenly there came a sound from heaven, as of a rushing mighty wind, and it filled the whole house where they were sitting. Then there appeared to them divided tongues, as of fire, and one sat upon each of them. And they were all filled with the Holy Spirit and began to speak with other tongues, as the Spirit gave them utterance.

Acts 2:1-4, NKJV

But Peter, standing up with the eleven, raised his voice and said to them, "Men of Judea and all who dwell in Jerusalem, let this be known to you, and heed my words. For these are not drunk, as you suppose, since it is *only* the third hour of the day. But this is what was spoken by the prophet Joel: 'And it shall come to pass in the last days, says God, That I will pour out of My Spirit on all flesh; Your sons and your daughters shall prophesy, Your young men shall see visions, Your old men shall dream dreams. And on My menservants and on My maidservants I will pour out My Spirit in those days; And they shall prophesy. I will show wonders in heaven above And signs in the earth beneath: Blood and fire and vapor of smoke. The sun shall be turned into darkness, And the moon into blood, Before the coming of the great and awesome day of the Lord. And it shall come to pass *That* whoever calls on the name of the Lord Shall be saved.'

Acts 2:14-21, NKJV

Jesus said He had to return to the Father so He could bestow on us the gift of the Holy Spirit. I think of the Holy Spirit as my secret weapon. In life when others are distressed, or storms are raging, we as Christians have the faith and hope that we have the third person of the Trinity—the Holy Spirit—who will speak to us, and guide and direct us.

In this story, Peter is preaching his first sermon after the infilling of the Holy Spirit. Many converts came to Jesus after hearing him speak. This was the same man Jesus had foretold would deny Him. "Now Simon Peter stood and warmed himself. Therefore they said to him, 'You are not also *one* of His disciples, are you?' He denied it and said, 'I am not!' One of the servants of the high priest, a relative *of him* whose ear Peter cut off, said, 'Did I not see you in the garden with Him?' Peter then denied again; and immediately a rooster crowed" (John 18:25-27, NKJV). Can you imagine being Peter and feeling the guilt of this betrayal? Jesus is so kind and loving that He restores Peter in John 15:15-19.

The power of the Holy Spirit is beautifully threaded throughout the New Testament. One of my favorite stories of Peter is found in Acts.

And through the hands of the apostles many signs and wonders were done among the people. And they were all with one accord in Solomon's Porch. Yet none of the rest dared join them, but the people esteemed them highly. And believers were increasingly added to the Lord, multitudes of both men and women, so that they brought the sick out into the streets and laid *them* on beds and couches, that at least the shadow of Peter passing by might fall on some of them. Also a multitude gathered from the surrounding cities to Jerusalem, bringing sick people and those who were tormented by unclean spirits, and they were all healed.

Acts 5:12-16, NKJV

I think this story should be an example of how your countenance can be transformed by the presence of the Holy Spirit in your life. There is a diversity of gifts of the Holy Spirit. The amazing gifts that God has given the church for edification and encouragement, and at times correction, can be found in 1 Corinthians 12.

There are diversities of gifts, but the same Spirit. There are differences of ministries, but the same Lord. And there are diversities of activities, but it is the same God who works all in all. But the manifestation of the Spirit is given to each one for the profit *of all*: for to one is given the word of wisdom through the Spirit, to another the word of knowledge through the same Spirit, to another faith by the same Spirit, to another gifts of healings by the same Spirit, to another the working of miracles, to another prophecy, to another discerning of spirits, to another *different* kinds of tongues, to another the interpretation of tongues. But one and the same

Spirit works all these things, distributing to each one individually as He wills.

1 Corinthians 12:4-11, NKJV

This is a beautiful medley of the individual notes that compose the symphony of the Holy Spirit in which each member plays their note through the Spirit and the song is beautifully displayed for all to gain understanding from the Father.

I would be remiss if I did not mention the attributes of the fruits of the spirit that as followers of Christ we should demonstrate in our lives each day. I wish that I could tell you these all come easily to me but that would be a lie. What am I talking about? Galatians 5 lists traits, or fruit, that should be produced in our lives for others to see.

> But the fruit of the Spirit is love, joy, peace, longsuffering, kindness, goodness, faithfulness, gentleness, self-control. Against such there is no law. And those *who are* Christ's have crucified the flesh with its passions and desires. If we live in the Spirit, let us also walk in the Spirit.

Galatians 5:22-25, NKJV

When you are in a room, listen to the voice of the Holy Spirit prompting you to speak to individuals that He wants you to minister to. Even your shadow can change the surroundings of those around you. What are you striving for? When you sit down in the boardroom or are walking down the aisle of your local grocery store, can people tell by your actions and deeds that you are a child of the King? Shouldn't they be able to?

8.

THE PROMISE OF THE MIRACLE-FILLED LIFE

What is a miracle to you? For me, a miracle is an unexpected, undeserving blessing that is God-breathed. If you are a parent, aunt, uncle, or grandparent you know exactly what I am talking about. The first look at a newborn baby you know that God is real and a good father. The majesty of creation daily reminds us how majestic and awesome He is.

> The heavens declare the glory of God; and the firmament show His handiwork.
>
> Psalms 19:1, NKJV

> When I consider Your heavens, the work of Your fingers, the moon and the stars, which You have ordained.
>
> Psalms 8:3, NKJV

I think the next verse is the most beautiful description of God's handy work.

> He who builds His layers in the sky, and has founded His strata in the earth; Who calls for the waters of the sea, and

pours them out on the face of the earth—the Lord is His
name.

Amos 9:6, NKJV

One of my favorite places to be in all the world is at the beach.
I love going there for several reasons, but one of my favorites
is that it makes me feel small. When I feel the warmth of the
sun and I take in the view of the ocean with the magnificent
waves rolling in it reminds me how massive and powerful the
God I love and serve is. If His words spoke this world into
creation, then how can I doubt His Word. "Then God said,
'Let there be a firmament in the midst of the waters, and let it
divide the waters from the waters'" (Genesis 1:6, NKJV). And
in verse 9, "Then God said, 'Let the waters under the heavens
be gathered together into one place, and let the dry *land* ap-
pear'; and it was so. And God called the dry *land* Earth, and
the gathering together of the waters He called Seas. And God
saw that *it was* good" (Genesis 1:9-10, NKJV).

Then in the New Testament Jesus reminds the disciples.

Then He said to His disciples, "Therefore I say to you, do
not worry about your life, what you will eat; nor about the
body, what you will put on. Life is more than food, and the
body is more than clothing. Consider the ravens, for they
neither sow nor reap, which have neither storehouse nor
barn; and God feeds them. Of how much more value are
you than the birds? And which of you by worrying can add

one cubit to his stature? If you then are not able to do the least, why are you anxious for the rest? Consider the lilies, how they grow: they neither toil nor spin; and yet I say to you, even Solomon in all his glory was not arrayed like one of these. If then God so clothes the grass, which today is in the field and tomorrow is thrown into the oven, how much more *will He clothe* you, O *you* of little faith?

Luke 12:22-28, NKJV

What is living a miracle-filled life? This does not mean you will have a life free of difficulties, but it is a life in which the presence of God is so evident that even if a situation is not working out in my favor, it can be turned around. And when I call on God, my Father, He hears and intervenes on my behalf. I would like to share with you one of the miracles I have personally experienced in my life.

My father was preaching a revival at a small country church in Pursglove, West Virginia. I became deathly ill. I had mono and strep throat, and my throat was almost swollen completely shut. My mom was rocking me one evening while my dad was preaching. I was about nine years old and my mom told me I needed to ask Jesus to heal me because He could. But also that I needed to use my faith. So, I prayed and started to sing the song, *He is All I Need*. The more I sang, the stronger I became, and at the end of the song I was completely restored.

The next day we went to church and my dad asked me to sing. I had never sung in front of anyone before, but I felt the prompting of the Holy Spirit. I went to the stage and sang Amazing Grace. I could not even believe it was me. God's presence filled the room as I obeyed my father and the prompting of that still small voice. I know a lot of people may not believe miracles are for today, but I am going to read the Word and stand on God's promise that He is the same today and forever. This is found in Hebrews, "Jesus Christ is the same yesterday, today, and forever" (Hebrews 13:8, NKJV). If the Bible says it then I am going to believe it. Search God's Word for yourself. Study and pray God will speak to your heart for your situation. Stand on His promises.

I would like to share one more encouragement with you. I was expecting our first child and probably about twenty weeks into my pregnancy for our Breanna Rose. I started bleeding and immediately went to the doctor. But before my mom and I left to go to the doctor we alerted our church family, and I called my husband and my sister. They immediately started bombarding heaven on my behalf. I have been so desperate that the only word I could get out of my mouth is "Jesus". He hears us and knows. The bleeding stopped before I arrived. This may be small to you but my miracle baby is twenty-two now.

To build faith to believe for miracles you need to read the Word, worship, and listen to the testimonies of others. The Bible is full of miracles from the parting of the Red Sea found in Exodus 14 to the awesome story of the walls coming down in Joshua 8. That story tells us that praise and worship are some of the greatest weapons. Verse 20 is the verse of victory that tells us the wall is falling flat. What is the wall in your life you are facing that you need God to bring down? What is your testimony? What has God done for you that you should share with someone to help build their faith? Be an encourager. Paul sent the letter to the church in Antioch. "So when they were sent off, they came to Antioch; and when they had gathered the multitude together, they delivered the letter. When they had read it, they rejoiced over its encouragement" (Acts 15:30-31, NKJV).

Then heading to chapter 19 is very thought-provoking: miracles glorify Christ. The purpose of miracles occurring is to draw individuals to Jesus. "Now God worked unusual miracles by the hands of Paul, so that even handkerchiefs or aprons were brought from his body to the sick, and the diseases left them and the evil spirits went out of them" (Acts 19:11-12, NKJV). Do you want to pursue God so much that when you walk into a room, or a piece of your clothing is sent to someone in the name of Jesus, they are set free?

9.

THE PROMISE OF PROVISION

As a parent, female, and wife there have been times when John and I wondered how we were going to make ends meet. I would pick up extra shifts and John would pick up the overtime shift as available. One thing I wish I would have taken hold of earlier in my walk with Jesus is to have the realization that if it is important to me, it is important to God. Just think about that for a minute. It is a powerful statement, is it not?

I am not just making a statement; I can back it up with scripture from God's Word. But first, let us take a minute to define what provision means. Webster's Dictionary defines provision as a measure taken beforehand to deal with a need, or a stock of needed materials or supplies. So, let us look at some miraculous type of provisions in scripture.

Provision of Supply: John 6. The back story of this scripture is that Jesus had been teaching and a great multitude had been following Him. His disciples told Jesus that the people were hungry. So, they were looking at natural means of how to feed the large crowd.

One of His disciples, Andrew, Simon Peter's brother, said to Him, "There is a lad here who has five barley loaves and two small fish, but what are they among so many?" Then Jesus said, "Make the people sit down." Now there was much grass in the place. So the men sat down, in number about five thousand. And Jesus took the loaves, and when He had given thanks He distributed *them* to the disciples, and the disciples to those sitting down; and likewise of the fish, as much as they wanted. So when they were filled, He said to His disciples, "Gather up the fragments that remain, so that nothing is lost." Therefore they gathered *them* up, and filled twelve baskets with the fragments of the five barley loaves which were left over by those who had eaten.

John 6:8-13, NKJV

I am so intrigued by this story for several reasons. I wonder if the parent, when they prepared the lunch for the day, told them to be sure they shared if someone did not have anything. Can you imagine when this little boy finally went home for the day the incredible story that he shared with his parents? We cannot also skip the amazing part that what is little and not enough in your hands is completely different than what the outcome is in Jesus' hands. He gave thanks and it multiplied. What area of your life do you feel you do not have enough? Are you willing to hand all that you have over to Jesus?

Provision of Protection: this provision is especially important for me. I live and work away from my family. My girls live several hours away from me. I pray blessings of protection over them daily. Psalms 91 is the promise I stand on daily for them and our family.

> He who dwells in the secret place of the Most High Shall abide under the shadow of the Almighty. I will say of the Lord, "*He is* my refuge and my fortress; My God, in Him I will trust." Surely He shall deliver you from the snare of the fowler *And* from the perilous pestilence. He shall cover you with His feathers, And under His wings you shall take refuge; His truth *shall be your* shield and buckler. You shall not be afraid of the terror by night, *Nor* of the arrow *that* flies by day, *Nor* of the pestilence *that* walks in darkness, *Nor* of the destruction *that* lays waste at noonday. A thousand may fall at your side, And ten thousand at your right hand; *But* it shall not come near you. Only with your eyes shall you look, And see the reward of the wicked. Because you have made the Lord, *who* is my refuge, *Even* the Most High, your dwelling place, No evil shall befall you, Nor shall any plague come near your dwelling; For He shall give His angels charge over you, To keep you in all your ways.
>
> Psalms 91:1-11, NKJV

This is a beautiful description of what your heavenly Father's love and protection look like. One of the things I loved so much about growing up was that my sister, Amy, and I always had confidence that from grade school all the way through high school our older brothers would protect us no matter what. We were blood and they would always have our backs. I always walked a little straighter and was happier knowing I had their love. Shouldn't we as Christians walk a little straighter and have a sense that we are children of the King? Does that mean we are not humble and love those who are hurting? Absolutely not. But those who are hurting should know that when we walk into the room, we are part of the solution. Like the little boy with the bagged lunch, we are bringing our gifts to Jesus for Him to multiply them.

God does ask for us to do our part. What does that mean? Well for the provision of supply, the Bible does tell us in 2 Chronicles 15:7, "But you, be strong and do not let your hands be weak, for your work shall be rewarded!" (NKJV). I think the story that best describes someone working diligently and it not working out like they anticipated is the story after Jesus died and was raised from the dead.

After these things Jesus showed Himself again to the disciples at the Sea of Tiberias, and in this way He showed *Himself*: Simon Peter, Thomas called the Twin, Nathanael of Cana in Galilee, the *sons* of Zebedee, and two others of His disciples were together. Simon Peter said to them, "I am going fishing." They said to him, "We are going with you also." They went out and immediately got into the boat, and that night they caught nothing. But when the morning had now come, Jesus stood on the shore; yet the disciples did not know that it was Jesus. Then Jesus said to them, "Children, have you any food?" They answered Him, "No." And He said to them, "Cast the net on the right side of the boat, and you will find *some*." So they cast, and now they were not able to draw it in because of the multitude of fish.

Therefore that disciple whom Jesus loved said to Peter, "It is the Lord!" Now when Simon Peter heard that it was the Lord, he put on *his* outer garment (for he had removed it), and plunged into the sea. But the other disciples came in the little boat (for they were not far from land, but about two hundred cubits), dragging the net with fish. Then, as soon as they had come to land, they saw a fire of coals there, and fish laid on it, and bread. Jesus said to them, "Bring some of the fish which you have just caught." Simon Peter went up and dragged the net to land, full of large fish, one hundred and fifty-three; and although there were so many, the net was not broken.

John 21:1-11

I have read this passage countless times. But I want to draw your attention to some beautiful truths that jumped off the page for me.

1. Always allow Jesus to be involved in every situation in your life and direct your path.

2. It takes your obedience and faith to change the circumstances. If the disciples had not had the faith to try it differently, they would have continued to come up

empty. I am so guilty of this in my career and in my personal life. I think it must have a lot to do with how I am made up. However, I am the only one limiting the potential of God moving in my life. If you want a different life or a greater revelation of who God is and what He can do in your life, get busy! Dive into His Word. Listen for His leading and act on it. Pray and worship and get with other Christians who are pursuing God as passionately, or more passionately, as you are.

3. I loved that in this version Jesus tells them they will find "some" of God's provision is not equal to our provision.

The disciples were overwhelmed with the harvest. Jesus referred to it as "some". This makes me laugh. We often look at our need in our humanness, but God wants us to see it through His eyes. The Bible tells us in Matthew:

Now if God so clothes the grass of the field, which today is, and tomorrow is thrown into the oven, *will He* not much more *clothe* you, O you of little faith? "Therefore do not worry, saying, 'What shall we eat?' or 'What shall we drink?' or 'What shall we wear?' For after all these things the Gentiles seek. For your heavenly Father knows that you need all these things. But seek first the kingdom of God and His righteousness, and all these things shall be added to you.

Matthew 6: 30-33, NKJV

God, who spoke the Word into existence, can speak life into whatever situation you are facing. He has provision for your health, job, financial situation, and spirit. There is no limit for Him. The fourth item that I loved in John verse 11 was dragging the net that was full of large fish and even though there were so many the net did not break. When the provision comes it stretches your ability to handle the blessing and promotion God has provided.

I would be remiss if in this chapter I did not talk about tithing. I am going to share from my own experience. When my husband and I first got married we had just started our careers. When we would look at the checkbook at the end of the week, I did not feel that we had enough to give God His portion. What a sad and immature mistake that was. I can tell you in our lives, since we recommitted our lives, time, hearts, and money to put everything in Godly submission and alignment with His Word we have been abundantly blessed. Does that mean we have never had challenges, lost a job, or had an unexpected expense come out of nowhere? The answer is no, but I do know one thing without a doubt: I have never been hungry, and I have never gone without.

I also love being generous. One of my favorite things to do is to send blessings to people. The unexpected card with encouragement, or a special gift to a child who may be strug-

81

gling. Or maybe even a stranger by buying their meal or leaving a waiter an amazing tip. Often, no one knows these things even occur. But I can picture my heavenly Father smiling in pleasure at the demonstration of His love. How can you help or bless someone? There is one thing I can tell you as a nurse who has worked with geriatric patients and terminally ill patients. You cannot take your money with you, but your impact on others and planting seeds of joy, encouragement, and love has a constant return and will impact generations to come. God's economy of reaping and sowing is beautiful, and you can never out-give Him. You can try but it will never happen.

Malachi has a beautiful scripture about God's economy, but it does come with a warning not to rob God.

"Will a man rob God? Yet you have robbed Me! But you say, 'In what way have we robbed You?' In tithes and offerings. You are cursed with a curse, For you have robbed Me, *Even* this whole nation. Bring all the tithes into the storehouse, That there may be food in My house, And try Me now in this," Says the Lord of hosts, "If I will not open for you the windows of heaven And pour out for you such blessing That *there will* not *be room* enough *to receive it.* "And I will rebuke the devourer for your sakes, So that he will not destroy the fruit of your ground, Nor shall the vine fail to bear fruit for you in the field," Says the Lord of hosts; "And all nations will call you blessed, For you will be a delightful land," Says the Lord of hosts.

Malachi 3:8-12, NKJV

We attend an amazing church that 100% believes God loves us so much and only wants the best for His children. The Bible tells us in Matthew 7:11 if we can give good gifts to our own children how much will God give us good gifts. That leaves me breathless. I cannot even put into words how much I love our girls. It brings tears to my eyes to think of how much God loves them and me.

10.

THE PROMISE OF ETERNITY

Iam so thankful for the promise of eternity and heaven. I would not have this promise of a reunion one day with loved ones without Jesus' death and resurrection. The key to this is salvation through the blood of Jesus.

> Who has saved us and called *us* with a holy calling, not according to our works, but according to His own purpose and grace which was given to us in Christ Jesus before time began, but has now been revealed by the appearing of our Savior Jesus Christ, *who* has abolished death and brought life and immortality to light through the gospel.
>
> 2 Timothy 1:9-10, NKJV

This promise is so very personal to me because even though I am only in my forties, my father has already been given the privilege of meeting Jesus face-to-face. The journey for my father was a remarkably interesting and trying journey. My father had dementia and as his disease progressed, we saw his once strong, vibrant, and very stocky body wither to a very weak shell of who he once was. But one thing that did not change was his love of the Lord. He may not have remembered how to read his Bible but my sister would put him in his chair and let him have his Bible.

I think one thing my sibling and our family held onto during this journey was that he was not scared. Death did not in the least frighten this man of God. He would often talk to us about us knowing that. He did not want us to waste our time visiting his grave and grieving over a shell, as he called it. He said, "Live and enjoy your life, but most of all serve Jesus so we can see each other soon."

He would tell us God's timing is not ours and it will just be a little while until we see him again. What a beautiful gift to be able to give your children and loved ones.

On the day of our daddy's death, it was kind of a rough day for him. We frequently had to give him medication to ensure he was comfortable. But I can tell you a beautiful feeling of peace was present in our home. No one will ever convince me that our beautiful blue-eyed hero did not see Jesus and immediately receive the reward he so longed for. I am so thankful for the moments of clarity that God provided to my dad so he could say goodbye and give instruction to us. What a gift. In Psalms 116:15 it says, "Precious in the sight of the Lord is the death of His saints" (NKJV). "Rejoice and be exceedingly glad, for great *is* your reward in heaven, for so they persecuted the prophets who were before you" (Matthew 5:12, NJKV).

What is in store for us? I am so glad you asked. No more tears. "He will swallow up death forever, And the Lord God will wipe away tears from all faces" (Isaiah 24:8, NKJV). As followers of Christ, we do not have to grieve like those who do not have the hope of eternity. This promise is found in Thessalonians:

> But I do not want you to be ignorant, brethren, concerning those who have fallen asleep, lest you sorrow as others who have no hope. For if we believe that Jesus died and rose again, even so God will bring with Him those who sleep in Jesus. For this we say to you by the word of the Lord, that we who are alive *and* remain until the coming of the Lord will by no means precede those who are asleep. For the Lord Himself will descend from heaven with a shout, with the voice of an archangel, and with the trumpet of God. And the dead in Christ will rise first. Then we who are alive *and* remain shall be caught up together with them in the clouds to meet the Lord in the air. And thus we shall always be with the Lord. Therefore comfort one another with these words.
>
> 1 Thessalonians 4:13-18, NKJV

This is known as the rapture of the church. One day that no one knows, Jesus will return for His people. Will you be ready? I know one thing is true for me personally, if I go through life and have a successful career and blessed life but one member of my family or friends misses spending eternity in heaven, I count it all a loss. What are you doing to add more to the eternal count of souls? Do not get so distracted with your goals that you do not remember to love on your family and make sure they are good spiritually.

Who is the person or persons that you long to see again? As you read this book, we may never have the pleasure on this earth to meet in person, but I would love to meet you one day this side of heaven or the other.

I leave you with some final closing questions to dwell on.

1. Are you preparing yourself to know God's promises?

2. Are you reading your Bible and praying each day?

3. Are you connected to your local church who challenges you to be better?

4. How are you serving your local church?

5. Who around you needs you to be Jesus to them?

6. When was the last day you took time to have an intimate conversation with Jesus and tell Him about your deepest secrets and dreams?